Fun Chinese New Year Crafts

W9-CEY-246

Karen E. Bledsoe

Enslow Elementary

an imprint of

Enslow Publishers, Inc.

E

40 Industrial Road
Box 398
Berkeley Heights, NJ 07922
USA

http://www.enslow.com

Enslow Elementary, an imprint of Enslow Publishers, Inc.
Enslow Elementary® is a registered trademark of Enslow Publishers, Inc.

Originally published as *Chinese New Year Crafts* in 2005.

Library of Congress Cataloging-in-Publication Data

Bledsoe, Karen E., author.
    [Chinese New Year crafts]
    Fun Chinese New Year crafts / Karen E. Bledsoe.
        pages cm. — (Kid fun holiday crafts!)
    "Originally published as Chinese New Year Crafts in 2005."
     Audience: K to grade 3.
    Includes bibliographical references and index.
    ISBN 978-0-7660-6240-5
    1. Chinese New Year decorations—Juvenile literature. 2. Chinese New Year—Juvenile literature. 3. Handicraft—Juvenile
        literature. I. Title.
    TT900.C38B54 2015
    745.594'161—dc23
                                            2014023468

Summary: "Explains the importance of Chinese New Year and how to make ten holiday-related crafts"—Provided by publisher.

Future editions:
Paperback ISBN: 978-0-7660-6241-2
EPUB ISBN: 978-0-7660-6242-9
Single-User PDF ISBN: 978-0-7660-6243-6
Multi-User PDF ISBN: 978-0-7660-6244-3

Printed in the United States of America

102014 Bang Printing, Brainerd, Minn.

10 9 8 7 6 5 4 3 2 1

To Our Readers: We have done our best to make sure all Internet addresses in this book were active and appropriate when we went to press. However, the author and the publisher have no control over and assume no liability for the material available on those Internet sites or on other Web sites they may link to. Any comments or suggestions can be sent by e-mail to comments@enslow.com or to the address on the back cover.

♻ Enslow Publishers, Inc., is committed to printing our books on recycled paper. The paper in every book contains 10% to 30% post-consumer waste (PCW). The cover board on the outside of each book contains 100% PCW. Our goal is to do our part to help young people and the environment too!

Illustration Credits: Crafts prepared by June Ponte; craft photography by Carl Feryok; Corel Corporation, p. 4; © 2004 Jupiter Images, p. 26 (animal illustrations).

Cover Illustration: Craft prepared by June Ponte; craft photography by Kristin McCarthy and Carl Feryok.

Contents

Safety Note: Be sure to ask for help from an adult, if needed, to complete these crafts!

INTRODUCTION

Boom go the fireworks! *Crash, clang* go the noisemakers! It is the first day of the first lunar month of the year. In China and most of Asia, that means it is New Year's Day! The lunar New Year begins between January 21 and February 19.

According to Chinese legend, dragons are good and powerful creatures that bring rain for the crops. In winter, China gets very little rain. Chinese people believe that the dragons are asleep during the New Year. The people make lots of noise on the first day of the New Year to drive away evil spirits and to wake the dragons.

People say, *"Gung hay fat choy"* to one another, which means, "Congratulations for coming into prosperity." Families gather for a feast. Some may have an eight-sided flat tray with sections for holding foods believed to bring luck. People may eat many symbolic foods: spring rolls that represent gold bricks, steamed clams for good fortune, and tangerines and oranges for luck.

On New Year's Day, people go to watch the Dragon Parade. Dancers carry huge dragon puppets through the streets. The dragons may spit fire from firecrackers in their mouths. Wherever the dragon goes, luck is said to follow.

The New Year celebration ends on the fifteenth day with the Lantern Festival. According to legend, the Jade Emperor was unhappy with a certain city and wanted the Fire Goddess to burn it. The wise man Donfang Shuo saved his city by giving the Fire Goddess her favorite food of sweet rice balls, which won her favor. He also had everyone in the city light lanterns and set off fireworks to fool the Jade Emperor into believing the city was on fire.

Today, people hang brightly colored paper lanterns. Some are simple while others are very fancy. Some are made to look like animals or flowers. At night there are parades with clowns, jugglers, and musicians. Sometimes there are dragon puppets. The best part of the celebration is the lion dance. Dancers carry huge lion puppets. One dancer carries a yellow ball that represents the sun, which the lion chases.

By the end of the festival, the dragons are awake, and the rains will soon come. People hope that all their celebrations will bring them good fortune for the rest of the year.

NEW YEAR BANNERS

The Chinese hang banners of red paper with poems or good luck symbols outside their doors. You can make your own banners and make them say, *"Gung hay fat choy."* It means, "Congratulations on coming into prosperity." By congratulating one another, the people are wishing prosperity on each other.

WHAT YOU WILL NEED

- red construction paper
- gold tissue paper
- scissors
- black tempera paint
- paper cup
- fine brush
- glue stick (not white glue)
- soda straw
- red, yellow, or black yarn or ribbon
- glitter (optional)

WHAT TO DO

1. Cut a strip of red paper the size of the banner you want. A nice size for a small banner is 2 inches wide by 5 inches long.

2. Mix one part tempera paint with one part water in a paper cup. Paint Chinese characters on the banner. Look on the next page for the characters for *"Gung hay fat choy."* Let dry.

3. Cut a piece of gold tissue paper about ¼-inch wider and 2 inches longer than the red paper.

4. Cover the back of the red paper with glue stick. Do not use white glue. It will not stick to the tissue paper. Stick the red paper onto the gold tissue paper so that one end of the red paper is ¼-inch from the end of the gold tissue paper. Let dry.

5. Wrap the short end of the tissue paper around a soda straw. Glue the end down on the back of the banner. Cut the ends of the soda straw even with the sides of the banner.

6. Cut a piece of yarn or ribbon three or four times as long as the width of the banner. Run the yarn or ribbon through the straw, and tie the ends in a knot.

Cut red and gold paper . . .

Write your message on the red paper and glue it to the gold one . . .

Carefully wrap the top of the gold paper around a straw . . .

If you wish, add glitter. Add a ribbon and your banner is ready to be hung up!

HOLIDAY HINT:

Hang these banners by your door or in your window to wish everyone prosperity.

CHUAN LIAN—
GOOD LUCK CHARACTERS

Many traditional Chinese people believe that one's luck during the year depends on what one does during the New Year celebrations. People hang good luck characters in their houses to bring good luck for the rest of the year.

WHAT YOU WILL NEED

- red or yellow construction paper
- gold or red tissue paper
- scissors
- black tempera paint
- fine brush
- glue stick (not white glue)
- fabric trim (optional)

WHAT TO DO

1. Cut a 4-inch square of red construction or tissue paper. Turn the square to make a diamond.

2. Thin the tempera paint using one part paint to one part water. Paint a good luck character on the red diamond. You can use the Chinese character on page 9. Let dry.

3. Cut a square piece of gold tissue paper or yellow construction paper about 4½ inches on each side. Spread glue stick on the back of the diamond, and glue to the tissue paper. Do not use white glue. It will peel off when dry. If you wish, decorate the edge with fabric trim.

4. When the glue is dry, trim the edges of the tissue paper so that about ¼-inch shows on all sides.

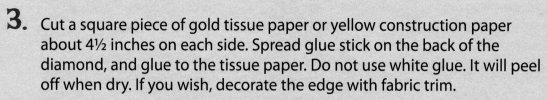

Start with a piece of square paper . . .

This is the Chinese character for good luck and fortune.

Glue it onto a piece of yellow paper. If you wish, add fabric trim.

HOLIDAY HINT:

With the help of an adult, find other good luck characters on the internet.

Chinese Zodiac Pictures

According to Chinese legend, Buddha called all the animals to him before he left the earth. Only twelve came. Buddha rewarded these twelve by naming years after them. Find out what Chinese zodiac sign belongs to the current year and make a banner with the year's animal. See page 26 for the Chinese zodiac animal characters.

What You Will Need

* red construction paper
* black tempera paint
* paper cup
* fine brush
* pencil
* pictures of Chinese zodiac animals
* gold glitter glue or glitter markers
* scissors
* glue

What To Do

1. Cut a strip of red paper about 4 inches by 8 inches.

2. Cut a 2-inch square of yellow paper. Turn to make a diamond. Mix one part tempera paint with one part water in a paper cup. Paint the character of the animal you want to represent on the yellow square. Let dry.

3. Glue the yellow diamond onto the red strip near the top.

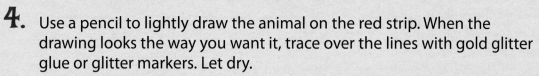

4. Use a pencil to lightly draw the animal on the red strip. When the drawing looks the way you want it, trace over the lines with gold glitter glue or glitter markers. Let dry.

5. If you like, make twelve banners to represent all the animals in the Chinese zodiac.

Start with red and yellow paper . . .

Draw a zodiac character . . .

Add ribbon and glitter . . .

Make one for each of the zodiac animals!

HOLIDAY HINT:

2015—Year of the Goat
2016—Year of the Monkey
2017—Year of the Rooster
2018—Year of the Dog
2019—Year of the Pig

Paper Firecracker Candy Holder

The Chinese set off firecrackers and fireworks on New Year's Eve to wake the dragons and to scare away evil.

What You Will Need

- toilet tissue roll
- red tissue paper
- string or yarn
- plastic wrap
- candy
- fine brush
- tape
- glitter pens or glitter glue

What To Do

1. Wrap a few pieces of candy loosely in a square of plastic wrap. Tie with a string, leaving about 6 inches of string extending from the candy bundle. Push the candy bundle inside of the toilet tissue roll so that the string hangs out. The end with the string is the top.

2. Cut a piece of red tissue paper about 7 inches by 12 inches. Place the tissue tube against the 7-inch edge so that the bottom end is about 1 inch from one edge of the red tissue. Carefully roll the tube up in the red tissue and tape the end. Turn the short ends under the bottom and tape in place.

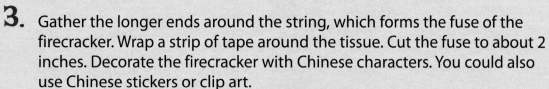

3. Gather the longer ends around the string, which forms the fuse of the firecracker. Wrap a strip of tape around the tissue. Cut the fuse to about 2 inches. Decorate the firecracker with Chinese characters. You could also use Chinese stickers or clip art.

Start with wrapping a toilet tissue roll with red tissue paper . . .

Wrap up some yummy candy . . .

Decorate the red tissue paper, and your firecracker is all finished!

HOLIDAY HINT:
Use these firecrackers as party favors. To get the candy out, pull on the "fuse" to tear the tissue.

Noisemakers

Chinese New Year celebrations are noisy! You can make safe and colorful noisemakers for your Chinese New Year parties.

What you will need

- small paper plates
- uncooked beans or unpopped popcorn
- red or yellow tissue paper
- colorful crepe paper
- glitter pens or glitter glue
- Chinese stickers or clip art (optional)
- stapler
- clear packing tape

What to do

1. Put about ten uncooked beans or unpopped popcorn kernels between two small paper plates. Staple the edges shut.

2. Cut a large piece of tissue paper, about 18 inches square. Place the noisemaker in the middle. Fold two sides of the paper around the noisemaker and tape in place. Fold the ends in, pulling the corners together to fit the round shape. Tape in place.

3. Cut three strips of crepe paper about 3 feet long. Glue them to the back in overlapping layers to cover the tape.

4. Decorate the front with stickers, clip art, or paint Chinese characters using glitter pens or glitter glue.

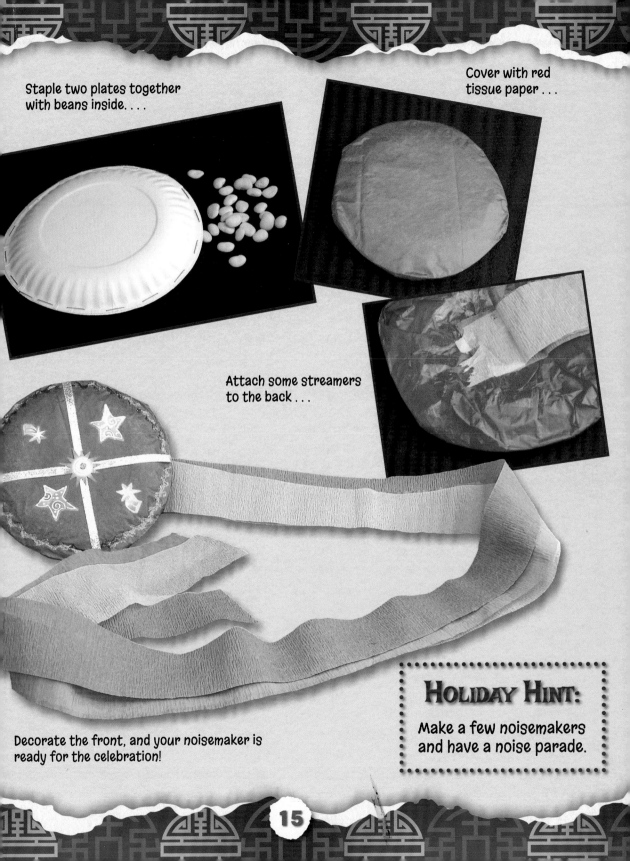

Staple two plates together with beans inside. . . .

Cover with red tissue paper . . .

Attach some streamers to the back . . .

Decorate the front, and your noisemaker is ready for the celebration!

HOLIDAY HINT:

Make a few noisemakers and have a noise parade.

DRAGON STREAMER PUPPET

Put on a New Year dragon parade with colorful puppets like this one. Use pictures of full-size Chinese dragon costumes to help you decorate your dragon.

WHAT YOU WILL NEED

* construction paper
* bright fluffy feathers or bright tissue paper
* crepe paper in bright colors
* scissors
* glue
* wiggle eyes

WHAT TO DO

1. Pick a piece of construction paper in a bright color. Fold the paper in half. Cut the corners opposite the fold to make them round. This is the dragon's head.

2. To make the dragon's mane, glue fluffy feathers along the folded edge. Or use fringed tissue paper. Cut construction paper about 2 inches wide and about the same width of the dragon's head. Cut long, curving points to look like eyebrows (or use the pattern on page 27). Glue in place to cover the ends of the feathers.

3. Cut two half-circles of paper for the eyes (pattern on page 27). Glue wiggle eyes to the half-circles. Glue some feather fluff to the backs of the eyes to make eyelashes. Glue the eyes below the eyebrows. Cut two shapes for nostrils (pattern on page 27). Glue in place.

4. For the dragon's whiskers, glue narrow feathers behind the nostrils. Cut six strips of crepe paper about 3 feet long. Glue to the underside near the folded edge, overlapping the strips. Cut a strip of paper about 1 inch wide and about the width of the head. Fold 1 inch under on either end. Glue the folded tabs to the underside of the head and let dry.

This is the handle for your puppet. Glue long strips of tissue paper under the bottom "lip" of the dragon to form the dragon's flames.

5. Let everything dry completely. When the puppet is ready, hold it by the handle and make it dance around.

Glue feathers along the top . . .

Fold a piece of construction paper in half . . .

Add the details for the face . . .

Add lots of streamers, and your puppet is done!

HOLIDAY HINT:

Turn your dragon into a lion by leaving off the flames and giving it a fluffy mane.

Dragon Costume

New Year's Day parades in China feature huge dragon costumes operated by several dancers. You can make your own dragon costume and put on a New Year parade.

What You Will Need

- brown paper bag
- scissors
- tape
- pencil
- stapler
- large sheets of construction paper
- crepe paper
- bright fluffy feathers
- markers
- white glue

What To Do

1. First, make a sturdy headband. Cut the bottom out of a brown paper bag. Cut up the seam and spread the paper out. Fold in half lengthwise, then fold in thirds lengthwise. Staple or glue in several places to hold the folds together.

2. Cut five pieces of crepe paper about 3 feet long. Glue these to the inside of the headband. Let dry. Wrap the headband around your head from back to front. Bring the ends flat against one another so that they stick out in front. Make a mark close to your head with a pencil. Remove the band and staple the band together where you made the pencil mark. Then, trim the ends to about 2 inches.

3. Draw a dragon head on a large piece of construction paper. Make the head about 18 inches long. Use the pattern on page 28 or make up your own dragon. Cut out the dragon head. Trace around the head on another piece of construction paper, and cut it out.

4. Lay the head shapes on your work surface with their noses facing each other. Decorate the heads. If you wish, cut teeth from white paper. Glue the teeth inside the mouth on one of the dragon heads. Glue a red feather in the dragon's mouth for a fluffy flame. Let the decorations dry completely.

5. Glue one head to one side of the headband, letting the snout stick out in front. The front extension on the headband helps support the dragon snout. Glue the other side of the head to the headband. Glue the two snouts together in front. Let dry completely.

6. Slip the headband on and you are ready for a dragon parade.

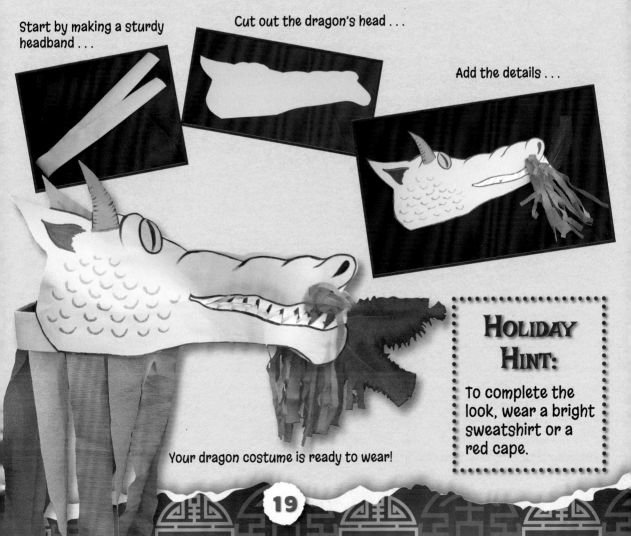

Start by making a sturdy headband . . .

Cut out the dragon's head . . .

Add the details . . .

Your dragon costume is ready to wear!

HOLIDAY HINT:

To complete the look, wear a bright sweatshirt or a red cape.

RED AND GOLD BRACELET

Red and gold are traditional colors symbolizing luck and prosperity to the Chinese. This bracelet features the New Year colors and is easy to make. It is one way to wear red on New Year's Eve as the Chinese do.

WHAT YOU WILL NEED

* red plastic pony beads or wooden beads

* metallic gold or yellow plastic pony beads or wooden beads

* ⅛-inch black elastic

* scissors

* craft glue (optional)

WHAT TO DO

1. Measure a piece of elastic that is as long as your wrist is around, plus 4 inches.

2. String the beads in a pleasing pattern. To look best, the pattern should have more red than gold. A pattern of two red beads, one gold bead, looks very nice.

3. As you string the beads, wrap the string around your wrist to see if the bracelet is long enough.

4. When the beads go around your wrist completely, tie the ends in a knot. For extra security, you can put a drop of craft glue on the knot.

5. Trim the ends of the elastic close to the knot, and your bracelet is ready to wear.

String them together . . .

Start with beads and elastic . . .

Carefully knot the ends . . .

Make lots for your family and friends!

HOLIDAY HINT:

Use black elastic because white is thought of as unlucky in China.

Ribbon Lantern

Here is an unusual lantern that makes a good decoration for the Lantern Festival. It takes time to tie all the knots, but the results are worth the effort.

What you will need

- two 6-inch paper plates
- red tempera paint (or any other bright color)
- brush
- hole punch
- scissors
- about 17-feet of brightly colored or metallic gold ¼-inch-wide satin or gift-wrap ribbon
- plastic beads (optional)

What to do

1. Paint both sides of the paper plates with tempera paint. Let dry completely.

2. Cut sixteen pieces of ribbon, each about 12 inches long. You can use one color for all ribbons, different colors for each ribbon, or make a pattern of various colors.

3. Use a hole punch to make sixteen holes evenly spaced around the edge of each plate.

4. Push the end of a ribbon through one of the holes so that the end sticks out of the bottom of the paper plate. Tie the end in an overhand knot. Do the same with the other fifteen ribbons. Add beads if you wish.

5. Push the ends of the ribbons through the holes in the second plate so that the ends stick out the bottom of the plate. Hold the lantern up and even out the bottom plate as much as possible, then tie the ends of the ribbons.

6. To make a handle, cut one more piece of ribbon about 12 inches long. Poke a hole in the center of one of the plates. Push both ends of the ribbon through the hole, from bottom to top. Tie the ends together in an overhand knot.

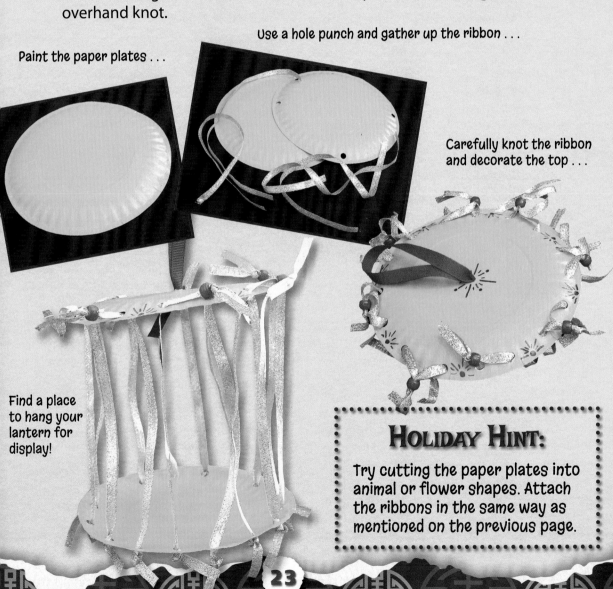

Use a hole punch and gather up the ribbon . . .

Paint the paper plates . . .

Carefully knot the ribbon and decorate the top . . .

Find a place to hang your lantern for display!

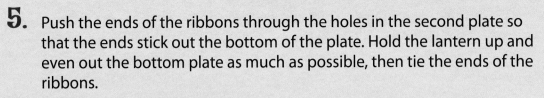

HOLIDAY HINT:

Try cutting the paper plates into animal or flower shapes. Attach the ribbons in the same way as mentioned on the previous page.

CHINESE PAPERCUTS

Chinese women often decorate their homes during the New Year with elaborate figures and scenes cut from black or colored paper. Try this simple craft to make a papercut panda.

WHAT YOU WILL NEED

- ❈ heavy white paper
- ❈ panda pattern
- ❈ scissors
- ❈ wiggle eyes (optional)

- ❈ glue
- ❈ black tempera paint (optional)

WHAT TO DO

1. Trace the panda pattern on page 29 onto heavy white paper. Cut the pattern out around the outline.

2. With scissors, carefully cut out the shaded parts of the pattern. To do this, make a snip in the middle of a shaded section. Cut to the edge of the shaded part, then slowly and carefully cut the shaded section out. Go slowly. Papercutting requires patience. The eyes are difficult to cut with scissors. Use a paper punch or leave uncut.

3. If you wish, place wiggle eyes or draw in eyes. Paint the ears, arms, and legs of the panda with black tempera paint.

4. Put your papercut up in a window for everyone to see.

Carefully cut the panda out . . .

Paint the ears, arms, and legs . . .

HOLIDAY HINT:

Make your own papercut using a different animal or other shape.

Your panda is all done!

PATTERNS

Use tracing paper to copy the patterns on these pages. Ask an adult to help you cut and trace the shapes onto construction paper.

Enlarge animals and symbols as needed

RAT OX TIGER RABBIT

DRAGON SNAKE HORSE GOAT

MONKEY ROOSTER DOG PIG

Enlarge to 110%

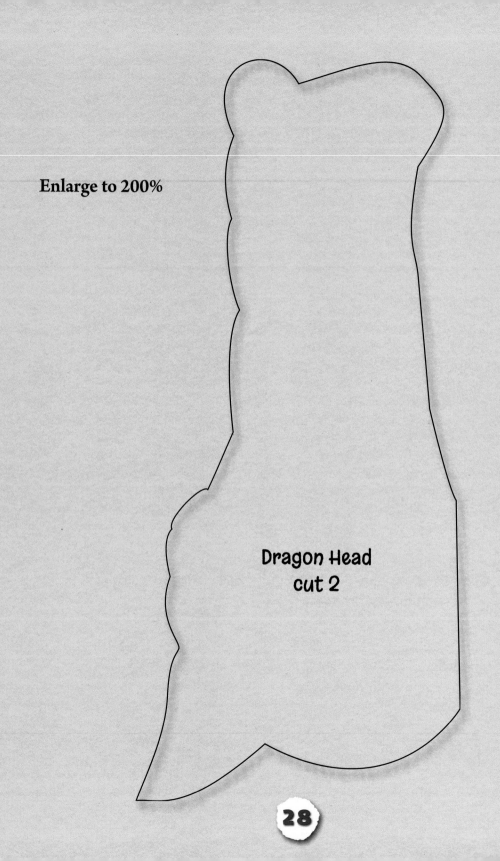

Enlarge to 200%

Dragon Head
cut 2

28

Enlarge to 110%

Cut out
shaded areas

29

Read About
Chinese New Year

Flanagan, Alice K. *Chinese New Year*. Minneapolis, Minn.: Compass Point Books, 2004.

Hoyt-Goldsmith, Diane. *Celebrating Chinese New Year*. New York: Holiday House, 1998.

Robinson, Fay. *Chinese New Year—A Time for Parades, Family, and Friends*. Berkeley Heights, N.J.: Enslow Publishers, Inc., 2001.

Simonds, Nina, and Leslie Swartz, and the Children's Museum of Boston. *Moonbeams, Dumplings & Dragon Boats: A Treasury of Chinese Holiday Tales, Activities & Recipes*. San Diego, Calif.: Harcourt, Inc., 2002.

Young, Ed. *Cat and Rat: The Legend of the Chinese Zodiac*. New York: Henry Holt, 1995.

INDEX